THUNDER AND LIGHTNING

Written by David Cutts • Illustrated by David Henderson

Consultant: Amie C. Gallagher, Producer and Education Coordinator
American Museum—Hayden Planetarium

Troll

A thunderstorm is coming. Do you see a flash of lightning?
Do you hear a crash of thunder?

Sometimes the lightning makes a zigzag pattern across the sky.

Sometimes it flashes along a forked path. At times, the thunder is low and rumbling. Other times, it booms like a cannon.

Long ago, people thought that thunder and lightning were caused by the gods.

The ancient Greeks believed there was a fire god who hammered thunderbolts and lightning streaks on his anvil in the heavens. Then he gave them to Zeus, the king of the gods, who hurled them at his enemies.

Today, scientists study thunder and lightning. We know a lot about lightning, but much is still not understood. From scientists' studies, we do know that thunder and lightning occur everywhere in the air around the Earth. We also know that lightning is always happening. It hits the ground about a hundred times each second. So even as you are reading this book, somewhere in the world lightning is striking.

Lightning happens everywhere—but what is lightning?

Lightning is a spark of electricity—a spark so big that it lights up the sky. Lightning bolts that travel from a cloud to the Earth may be as long as 9 miles (14 kilometers).

Benjamin Franklin, a famous American who lived during Colonial times, proved that lightning is made of electricity.

In 1752, he tried an experiment with lightning. He tied some wire to a kite. Then he tied a key to the end of the kite string. He flew the kite in a thunderstorm. Electricity traveled from the storm clouds to the wire on the kite. Then it moved through the kite and down the kite string to the key. Franklin got quite a shock when a spark jumped from the key to his hand!

Benjamin Franklin's experiment with lightning was dangerous. To keep from being hit by lightning, we should never go outside during a thunderstorm. But there is a safe "lightning" experiment that you can try.

Just scuff your feet several times on a thick carpet. Then touch something made of metal. ZZZZZZZT! Did you get a tiny shock?

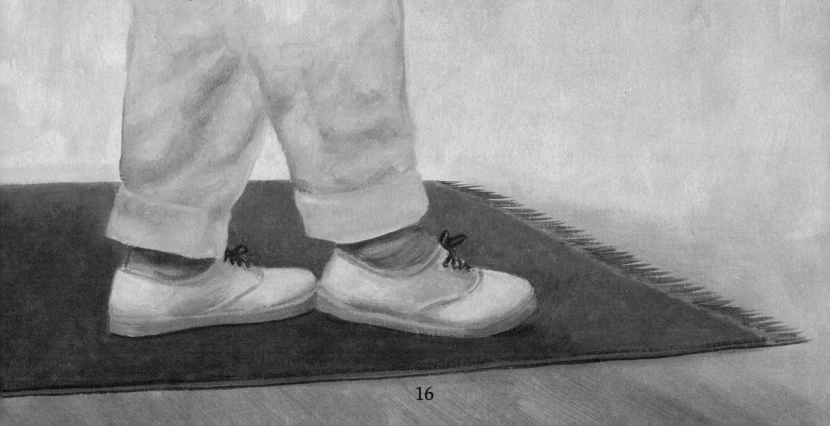

Did a small spark of "lightning" jump from your hand to the metal?

Why will a spark jump from your hand? Scuffing along a carpet builds up an electrical charge on you. Then the electrical charge discharges—it jumps from your hand to the metal you touched.

Here is how Benjamin Franklin's experiment was similar to yours. Electricity that had built up in the clouds traveled down Franklin's kite string to his key. Then it discharged from the key—and it jumped to Franklin's hand. In your experiment, the built-up charge discharged from your hand to the metal.

Lightning can jump in several ways. Sometimes it stays inside a cloud when it jumps. Or it may jump from one cloud to another. Other times lightning jumps out of a cloud and shoots across the sky.

And yet other times it jumps toward the ground.

Why does electricity build up in the clouds? Many scientists believe this happens because the tiny drops of water in the clouds have an electric charge.

As the drops move through the clouds, the electric charge builds up and becomes larger. Then, suddenly, the electricity discharges in a flash of lightning.

When electricity flashes from a cloud, it looks like one giant bolt of lightning. But the flash you see is really made up of several parts called lightning strokes. These strokes occur so quickly that they appear to flash all at the same time.

Sometimes streak lightning, which looks like a single jagged flash, turns into another kind of lightning. It looks like links in a chain, or beads on a string. This sort of lightning is called chain, or bead, lightning.

Some lightning follows two or more paths through the air.
When it branches out, or forks, it is called forked lightning.

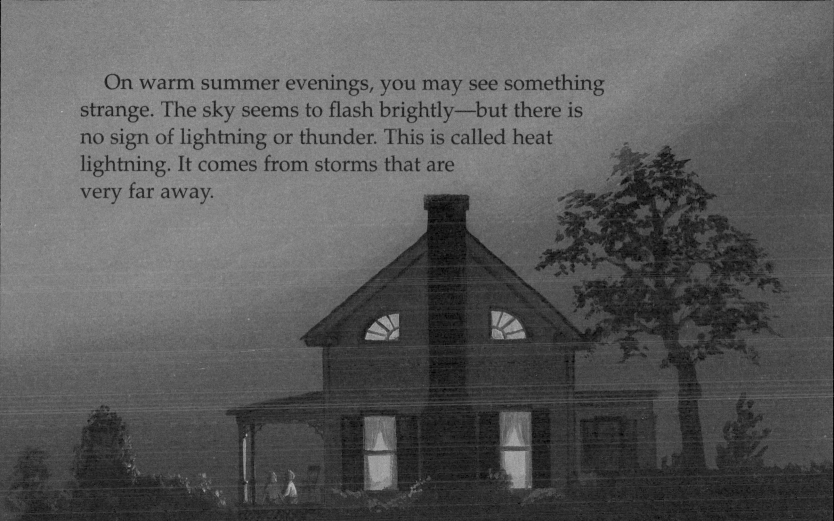

On warm summer evenings, you may see something strange. The sky seems to flash brightly—but there is no sign of lightning or thunder. This is called heat lightning. It comes from storms that are very far away.

Another strange sight is lightning with no flash at all. This is called Saint Elmo's fire. During stormy weather, this type of lightning looks like a glow on the top of a tall, pointed object, such as a ship's mast. Saint Elmo's fire has also been seen around the wings of airplanes that are traveling through storm clouds. Such lightning occurs when an electrical charge builds up on a pointed object and leaks away into the air.

Saint Elmo was a favorite saint of sailors long ago. When they saw Saint Elmo's fire on the top of a ship's mast, the sailors thought it was a sign of good luck.

Did you know that lightning causes thunder?

When lightning flashes through the air, the temperature of the air heats up. The hot air quickly expands, or flies out, and bangs into cooler air nearby. The moving air creates sound waves that rush away from the lightning flash. When the sound waves reach your ears, you hear thunder.

Thunder from nearby lightning sounds loud and sharp. This is called a thunderclap. When lightning is far away, you may hear only a distant booming sound.

Another kind of thunder is called long thunder. Long thunder makes a rolling, rumbling sound. It is often caused by a thunderclap that is echoing across the countryside.

Loud thunder and bright flashes of lightning can be exciting. But they can also be scary. And lightning can be dangerous. It can melt solid metal objects. It can split big trees apart. And it can hurt, or even kill, people.

How can we protect ourselves?

One safety device is a lightning rod. A lightning rod can attract lightning and make the lightning follow a safe path. Benjamin Franklin invented the first lightning rod many years ago. He put a metal rod on the roof of his house. A wire ran down to another metal rod that was stuck deep into the ground.

When lightning struck, it took the easy path to the ground—down the rod and wire—and its electricity went safely into the earth. Today similar lightning rods are still used on houses.

A tall steel building is like a giant lightning rod. The building has many metal parts that connect it to the ground. When lightning strikes, it passes through the metal and harmlessly into the ground.

Here are some safety rules to remember during a thunderstorm:

Do stay inside a house or car.

Do stay in a low place—away from metal fences—if you cannot reach shelter.

Don't stay under a tree, especially one that is standing by itself.

Don't stand near water.

Don't go swimming, boating, or into a bath or shower.

When you are in a safe place, a storm can be exciting. It can be fun to figure out how far you are from a flash of lightning.

Here's how to do it. First, count the seconds between the flash of lightning and the crash of thunder. Then divide that number by five to find the distance in miles. Or you can divide by three to find the distance in kilometers.

Look! Listen! A thunderstorm is coming. What kind of lightning is that? How far away is it?

Let's observe one of nature's most awesome wonders—the fireworks of thunder and lightning!